The Cyber Ghost Crew!

A Cyber Safety Adventure

By Jayme Simmons

The Cyber Ghost Crew!

Second Edition
First published in 2025

ISBN: 978-1-972486-03-0

Written by Jayme Simmons

Published by ChronoCipher Media
Colorado Springs, Colorado

Printed in the United States of America

Written by
Jayme Simmons

The screen glowed bright late into the night,
a boy clicked some links that looked
"just right."
He laughed and he typed,
with a snack in his hand,
Not knowing what trouble was close at hand!

FREE
COOKIES!

Then WHOOSH came a whirly,

a spark and a crash.

Three ghosts tumbled in with a boom and a

SMASH!

They tripped and they tumbled,

they squeaked

and they squealed,

a very odd trio of cyber-ghosts revealed!

Meet Phishy

"I'm Phishy!" one shouted, his hat with a hook,
with letters and spam spilling out of a book.
"Click silly links and I'll slip through with ease!
I'll steal cookies, passwords, and digital keys!"
I ride on fake emails, I *look* real, you see
Then grab all your secrets
and giggle with glee!"

CLICK
ME!

Phishy's Trick

Once you clicked 'OK!'
you thought you had won.
But the prize was a trap,
and the mischief was done!
I sneak in past your filters,
when you're careless
and quick!
I'm the sneakiest ghost of
a phishing old trick!"

YOU WON
A PONY
OK

Meet Patchy

"I'm Patchy!" yelled ghost two,

with tape in his hand,

"I patch up the software when hackers attack.

But if you don't update, I can't plug the hole,

and malware will dance on your files,

taking a toll!"

UPDATE NOW
PATCH ME!
UPDATE NOW
UPDATE NOW

Patchy's Warning

"Right now your poor laptop
is coughing and slow,
I see updates were skipped
many days in a row.
I patch and I plaster, but oh what a chore!
Your apps keep collapsing
right onto the floor!"

UPDATE
NOW

Meet Ransom Wreck

The last ghost was clumsy,
he tripped with a crash.
His pockets were jingling
with padlocks and cash.
"I'm Ransom Wreck! I'm your future, you see...
If you don't learn your lessons,
you'll soon deal with me!"

PAY 100 CANDY BARS!
PAY 100 CANDY BARS!
PATCH! ME!

Ransom Wreck's Chaos

"I'll lock up your homework,
your games, and your toys,
and demand chocolate payment
from all girls and boys!
Your bike will freeze up,
your robot won't walk,
your sneakers will clatter,
your laptop is locked!"

PAY
100
CANDY
BARS!

The three ghosts together
were noisy and loud.
They tripped over cables,
they stumbled around.
They bickered and bonked
in a wild cyber fight,
but taught the young boy,
what to do to be right.

Lesson One

Make passwords long,
don't be lazy, my friend!
Use letters, numbers & symbols
from start to end.
birthdays or '1234' will be tested.
Make passwords real tough so bad guys quit
when they're bested!

M0m&Dd4R#1!

Lesson Two

Keep updates turned on,
don't forget or delay!
Let Patchy keep bugs and bad glitches away.
When updates are ready,
just click and say 'yes,'
and your apps will stay healthy,
your stress will be less!

SECURE

Lesson Three

Never click links that look fishy or fake,

they're traps full of trouble,

avoid them for safety's sake.

If something seems odd or too good to be true,

remember that hackers are phishing for you!

FREE
PIZZA!

Final Warning

Protect all your secrets, your photos, your stuff,
The future is safe if you're careful enough.
But if you forget
and just click without care,
Ransom Wreck's waiting to give you a scare!

CHOC
Candy

The boy nodded quick, with a smile ear to ear,

"I'll be cyber-smart! Hackers won't come near!

Strong passwords, updates,

no clicking on trash,

I'll guard all my secrets and save all my stash!"

The ghosts gave a bow,
with a stumble and cheer,
then WHOOSH they spun off
till they all disappeared.
They bumbled and tripped,
they were silly, not mean,
the goofiest ghosts the kid ever had seen!

The boy closed the laptop,

switched off the bright light,

And drifted to sleep in the comfort of night.

With dreams full of coding

and passwords secure,

the boy was protected... of that we are sure!

Cyber Safety Review

- Don’t click strange links
- Keep your computer updated
- Back up your files
- Tell an adult if something feels wrong

The End

Also by Jayme Simmons

Malware Monster Mythology

Clix the Cat: Password Chaos (Book 1)

The Cyber Time Tracker Series

Follow Codey and Cypher as they travel through time to face the biggest digital threats in history. Each adventure helps young readers learn how technology works—and how smart choices help keep the digital world safe.

Book 1 – Codey's Malware Mission
Book 2 – Codey and the Speed of Worms
Book 3 – Codey and the Phishing Phantoms
Book 4 – Codey vs. the Ransomware Lock
Book 5 – Codey Battles the Botnet

Made in United States
North Haven, CT
05 November 2026

21765511R00022